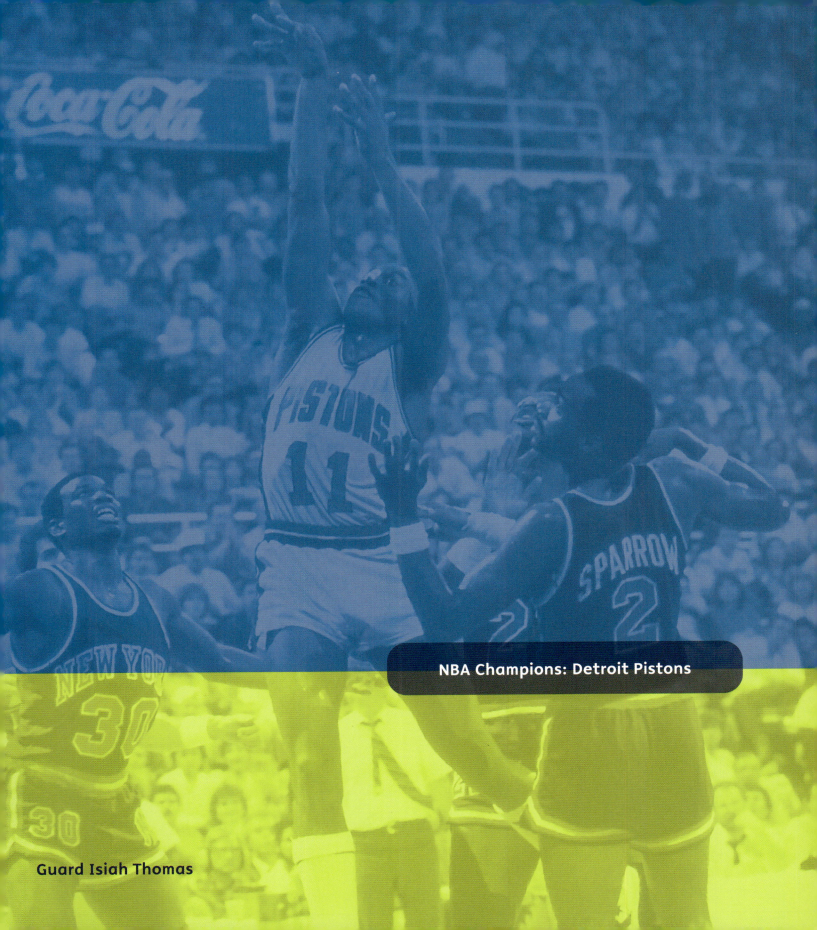

NBA Champions: Detroit Pistons

Guard Isiah Thomas

Guard Eric Money

NBA CHAMPIONS

DETROIT PISTONS

DENNY BULCAO, JR.

CREATIVE EDUCATION / CREATIVE PAPERBACKS

Guard Richard Hamilton

Published by Creative Education and Creative Paperbacks
P.O. Box 227, Mankato, Minnesota 56002
Creative Education and Creative Paperbacks are imprints of
The Creative Company
www.thecreativecompany.us

Art Direction by Tom Morgan
Book production by Graham Morgan
Edited by Grace Cain

Images by Associated Press/Carlos Osorio, cover; Getty Images/Allen Einstein,
4, Andrew D. Bernstein, cover, Andy Hayt, 3, Bettmann, 12, David E. Klutho,
24, Dick Raphael, 2, 6, 19, Doug Pensinger, 1, George Long, 15, Harry How, 10,
Icon Sports Wire, 16, Jason Miller, 5, Nic Antaya, 20; Newscom/Chris Szagola, 7;
Unknown, 9
Every effort has been made to contact copyright holders for material
reproduced in this book. Any omissions will be rectified in subsequent printings
if notice is given to the publisher

Copyright © 2025 Creative Education, Creative Paperbacks
International copyright reserved in all countries. No part of
this book may be reproduced in any form without written
permission from the publisher.

Library of Congress Cataloging-in-Publication Data

Names: Bulcao, Denny Jr., author.
Title: Detroit Pistons / by Denny Bulcao Jr.
Description: Mankato, Minnesota : Creative Education and Creative
   Paperbacks, [2025] | Series: Creative sports: NBA champions | Includes
   index. | Audience: Ages 7-10 | Audience: Grades 2-3 | Summary:
   "Elementary-level text and dynamic sports photos highlight the NBA
   championship wins of the Detroit Pistons, plus sensational players
   associated with the professional basketball team such as Cade
   Cunningham"— Provided by publisher.
Identifiers: LCCN 2024014024 (print) | LCCN 2024014025 (ebook) | ISBN
   9798889892557 (library binding) | ISBN 9781682776216 (paperback) | ISBN
   9798889893660 (ebook)
Subjects: LCSH: Detroit Pistons (Basketball team)—History—Juvenile
   literature. | Basketball players—United States—Juvenile literature.
Classification: LCC GV885.52.D47 B85 2025 (print) | LCC GV885.52.D47
   (ebook) | DDC 796.3230977434—dc23/eng/20240405
LC record available at https://lccn.loc.gov/2024014024
LC ebook record available at https://lccn.loc.gov/2024014025

Printed in China

Guard Reggie Jackson

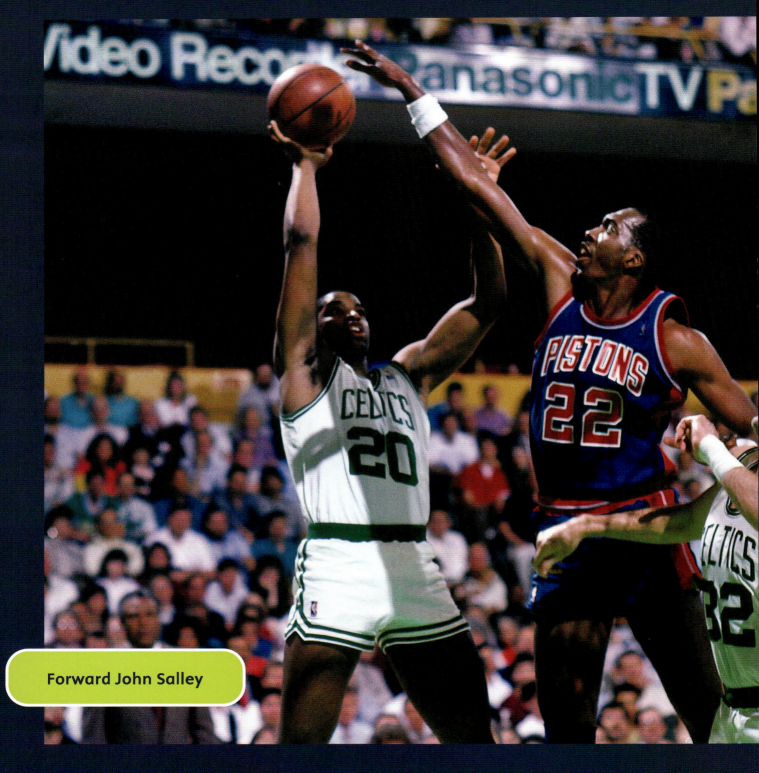

Forward John Salley

CONTENTS

Home of the Pistons	8
Naming the Pistons	11
Pistons History	13
Other Pistons Stars	18
About the Pistons	22
Glossary	23
Index	24

Home of the Pistons

Detroit is the largest city in Michigan. It is often called "The Motor City." It is where many cars were built. Detroit has a large building called Little Caesars **Arena**. It is home to the Pistons basketball team.

The Detroit Pistons are a National Basketball Association (NBA) team. They compete in the Central Division. That's part of the Eastern Conference. Two of their big **rivals** are the Chicago Bulls and Cleveland Cavaliers. All NBA teams want to win the **NBA Finals** and become champions.

NBA CHAMPIONS

Center Andre Drummond

Naming the Pistons

The first owner of the team was Fred Zollner. He had a company that made car parts. A piston is a major part of a car engine. The team was first called the Fort Wayne Zollner Pistons. When they moved to Detroit, they became the Detroit Pistons. The name worked well with the city's history.

Guard Gene Shue

Pistons History

The Pistons first started playing professionally in 1941 in the National Basketball League. They switched organizations in 1948. Guard Bobby McDermott was their first star. He sank basket after basket using a two-handed shot. The team reached the Finals in 1955 and 1956. They lost each time.

The team moved to Detroit in 1957. One special player was Dave DeBusschere. He was both a player and a coach when he was just 24 years old!

The Pistons became a top team in the 1980s under famous coach Chuck Daly. They played tough defense behind big, strong center Bill Laimbeer. They were nicknamed the "Bad Boys." Point guard Isiah Thomas led them to three straight NBA Finals. The team won **titles** in 1989 and 1990!

Forward Dave DeBusschere

DETROIT PISTONS

Guard Chauncey Billups

DETROIT PISTONS

The Pistons reached the Finals again in 2004 behind legendary coach Larry Brown. They won another championship by beating the Los Angeles Lakers. Chauncey Billups led the team. He was called "Mr. Big Shot" because he made many important baskets. The Pistons reached the Finals again in 2005. They lost to the San Antonio Spurs.

Other Pistons Stars

Guard Dave Bing was a top player in the 1960s and '70s. Bing's teammate, center Bob Lanier, was famous for his left-handed hook shots.

Guard Dave Bing

19

NBA CHAMPIONS

Point guard Cade Cunningham

DETROIT PISTONS

Forward Dennis "The Worm" Rodman was the best rebounder of the "Bad Boys." Ben Wallace was named the NBA's Defensive Player of the Year four times in the 2000s!

The Pistons haven't won a playoff game since 2008. They are looking to coach Monty Williams and point guard Cade Cunningham to turn things around.

About the Pistons

First season: 1941–42

Conference/division: Eastern Conference, Central Division

Team colors: royal blue, red, gray, navy blue, and white

Home arena: Little Caesars Arena

NBA CHAMPIONSHIPS:

1989, 4 games to 0 over Los Angeles Lakers

1990, 4 games to 1 over Portland Trail Blazers

2004, 4 games to 1 over Los Angeles Lakers

TEAM WEBSITE:

https://www.nba.com/pistons/

Glossary

Arena—a large building with seats for spectators, where sports games and entertainment events are held

NBA Finals—a series of games between two teams at the end of the playoffs; the first team to win four games is the champion

Rival—a team that plays extra hard against another team

Title—another word for championship

Center Ben Wallace

Index

Billups, Chauncey, 16, 17
Bing, Dave, 18, 19
Brown, Larry, 17
Cunningham, Cade, 20, 21
Daly, Chuck, 14
DeBusschere, Dave, 14, 15
Laimbeer, Bill, 14
Lanier, Bob, 18
Little Caesars Arena, 8, 22
McDermott, Bobby, 13
Rodman, Dennis, 21
team name, 11
Thomas, Isiah, 14
Wallace, Ben, 21
Williams, Monty, 21
Zollner, Fred, 11